SCIENCE SL...

?

SHARE IT!

AZZA SHARKAWY

Crabtree Publishing Company

www.crabtreebooks.com

SCIENCE SLEUTHS

?

Author
Azza Sharkawy

Publishing plan research and development
Reagan Miller

Editor
Shirley Duke, Reagan Miller, Kathy Middleton

Proofreader and indexer
Wendy Scavuzzo

Photo research
Katherine Berti

Design
Katherine Berti

Print and production coordinator
Katherine Berti

Illustrations
Bonna Rouse: p. 12 (life cycle); p. 17 (honeybee)
Katherine Berti: front cover (illustration)

Photographs
iStock: ShikharBhattarai p 20; p. 10
Shutterstock: ChameleonsEye p. 6
Thinkstock: title page
Wikimedia Commons: Wellcome Images p. 8 (left); p8 (right)

All other images by Shutterstock

Library and Archives Canada Cataloguing in Publication

Sharkawy, Azza, author
    Share it! / Azza Sharkawy.

(Science sleuths)
Includes index.
Issued in print and electronic formats.
ISBN 978-0-7787-0781-3 (bound).--ISBN 978-0-7787-0818-6 (pbk.).--
ISBN 978-1-4271-7715-5 (pdf).--ISBN 978-1-4271-7709-4 (html)

    1. Communication in science--Juvenile literature. 2. Report
writing--Juvenile literature. I. Title.

Q223.S43 2014   j501.4   C2014-903944-1
                                       C2014-903945-X

Library of Congress Cataloging-in-Publication Data

Sharkawy, Azza, author.
 Share it! / Azza Sharkawy.
    pages cm. -- (Science sleuths)
 Includes index.
 ISBN 978-0-7787-0781-3 (reinforced library binding) -- ISBN 978-0-7787-0818-6
(pbk.) -- ISBN 978-1-4271-7715-5 (electronic pdf) -- ISBN 978-1-4271-7709-4
(electronic html)
1. Communication in science--Juvenile literature. 2. Science--Methodology--
Juvenile literature. 3. Research--Juvenile literature. I. Title.

 Q223.S436 2015
 507.2'1--dc23
                            2014032326

Crabtree Publishing Company

www.crabtreebooks.com   1-800-387-7650

Printed in Canada/102014/EF20140925

Published in Canada
Crabtree Publishing
616 Welland Ave.
St. Catharines, Ontario
L2M 5V6

Published in the United States
Crabtree Publishing
PMB 59051
350 Fifth Avenue, 59th Floor
New York, New York 10118

Published in the United Kingdom
Crabtree Publishing
Maritime House
Basin Road North, Hove
BN41 1WR

Published in Australia
Crabtree Publishing
3 Charles Street
Coburg North
VIC 3058

CONTENTS

Two heads are better than one   4

Recording and sharing observations   6

Science notebooks   8

Why do scientists share?   10

How do scientists share?   12

Get graphing!   14

Picture this!   16

Write like a scientist   18

Present it!   20

Citizen scientists   22

Learning more   23

Glossary   24

Index   24

TWO HEADS ARE BETTER THAN ONE

Science is the study of the **natural world**. The natural world is made up of **living** things such as plants and animals. It is also made up of **non-living** things, such as rocks and rivers. People who study science are called **scientists**. Scientists **observe** to learn about the world around them.

*You use your **senses** when you see, smell, hear, taste, and touch!*

Scientists ask questions and look for possible answers. Scientists often work together. Working together and sharing information help scientists discover new things. The scientists below found a skeleton of an animal buried deep under the ground. They have many questions! They will work together to find the answers.

What kind of animal is it?

How long has it been buried?

RECORDING AND SHARING OBSERVATIONS

Scientists **investigate** to find answers to their questions. How scientists investigate depends on the types of questions they want to answer. Scientists sometimes ask questions that can be answered by doing research. Scientists research by reading books, searching the Internet, or talking with other scientists. For example, questions such as "Why is the sky blue?" and "What happened to the dinosaurs?" can be answered by reading books or talking with **experts**.

Some questions can be answered by doing an **experiment**. An experiment is an investigation that tests a **prediction**. A prediction is a possible answer to a question. Scientists use what they know about the question to make a prediction. They test their prediction and collect information. They use that information to decide if the results support their prediction. Finally, they share what they learned.

These children are doing an experiment to test what makes plants grow faster: water or milk. They predict that the plant given milk will grow fastest. They will test their prediction and share what they learned.

water

milk

SCIENCE NOTEBOOKS

Science notebooks are important tools. Scientists use notebooks to **record** their questions and **observations**, plan investigations, and organize **data**. Data is information collected during an investigation.

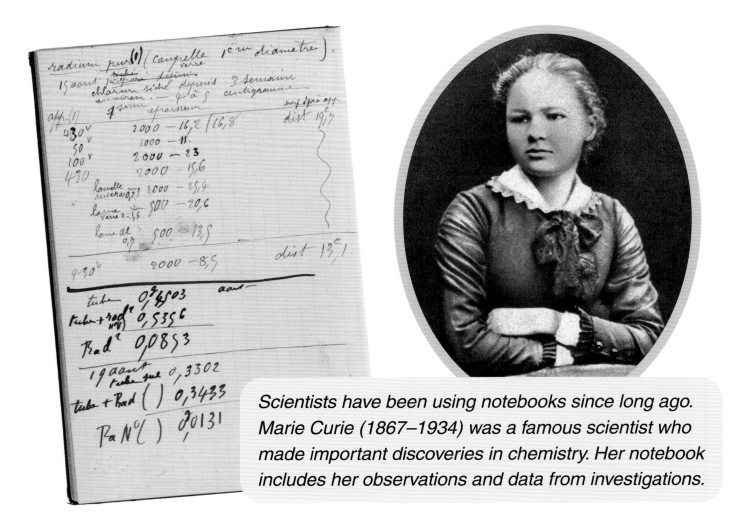

Scientists have been using notebooks since long ago. Marie Curie (1867–1934) was a famous scientist who made important discoveries in chemistry. Her notebook includes her observations and data from investigations.

Scientists take care to carefully record their observations and other notes in their notebooks. They add a lot of details when describing what they observe. They share this information with other scientists. It is important that their notes are clear and **accurate**, or correct.

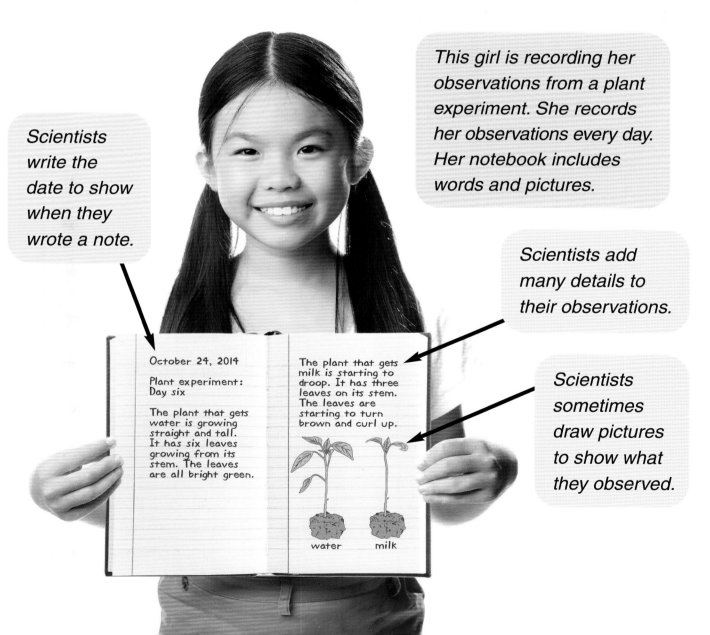

This girl is recording her observations from a plant experiment. She records her observations every day. Her notebook includes words and pictures.

Scientists write the date to show when they wrote a note.

Scientists add many details to their observations.

Scientists sometimes draw pictures to show what they observed.

October 24, 2014

Plant experiment: Day six

The plant that gets water is growing straight and tall. It has six leaves growing from its stem. The leaves are all bright green.

The plant that gets milk is starting to droop. It has three leaves on its stem. The leaves are starting to turn brown and curl up.

water   milk

WHY DO SCIENTISTS SHARE?

Communication is a big part of a scientist's job. Scientists spend a lot of time sharing information, asking questions, and reviewing each other's work.

Communicating, or sharing information, is an important part of science. To **communicate** means to write, draw, or speak to show what you have learned. Scientists share the results of their investigations and learn from each other. Information shared by one scientist can help another scientist. Some science discoveries may never have happened if scientists did not share information.

Scientists also share their work so that other scientists can review it. Scientists review and ask questions about the results of other scientist's work. They ask questions to make sure the scientist's data is accurate. Scientists can also check a scientist's work by repeating the investigation to see if they get the same results.

Reading, writing, speaking, and listening are all part of communication.

HOW DO SCIENTISTS SHARE?

Scientists record and share information in different ways. They do their best to record information in a way that is clear and organized so other people can understand it. They use words, pictures, and numbers to share information. How they record information depends on the kind of data they collected during their investigation. **Graphic organizers** are used to organize observations. Different ones can be used to show different kinds of data.

SEQUENCE CHART

A sequence chart is a graphic organizer used to place objects or events in order. This sequence chart shows the life cycle of a frog.

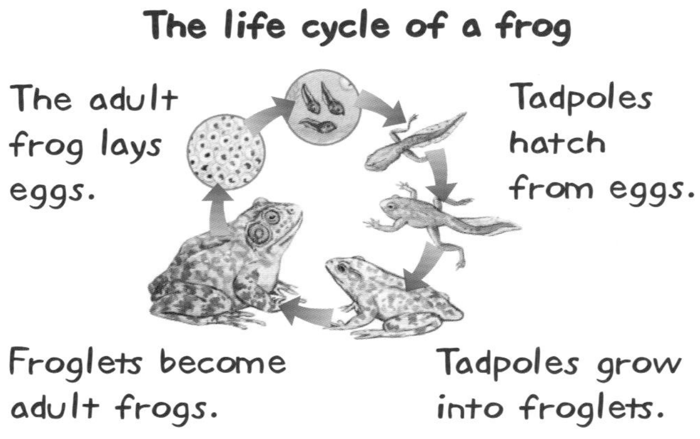

The life cycle of a frog

The adult frog lays eggs.

Tadpoles hatch from eggs.

Tadpoles grow into froglets.

Froglets become adult frogs.

VENN DIAGRAM

A Venn diagram is used to compare two or more things. To compare means to show how things are alike and how they are different. This girl asked "How is what I see in the daytime sky different from what I see in the nighttime sky?"

She observed the sky during the day and again at night. She recorded her observations on a Venn diagram.

EXPLORE IT!

Use the Venn Diagram to answer this question: What objects can be seen during the day and at night?

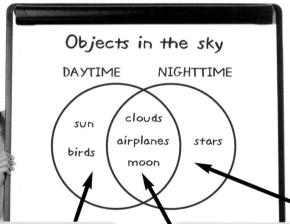

Objects in the sky

DAYTIME   NIGHTTIME

sun   clouds
birds   airplanes   stars
         moon

This part of the circle shows what she observed in the sky during the day.

This part of the diagram shows objects that can be observed both during the day and at night.

This part of the circle shows what she observed in the sky at night.

GET GRAPHING!

Charts and graphs help organize measurements and other number data. Graphs are drawings that use lines or bars to show data. Scientists must understand how to read the information. They must also know how to create graphs to show their own data.

LINE GRAPH

A line graph is a tool you can use to compare changes in data over time.

The lines connecting the dots help show if the data is going up, down, or staying the same. Use the graph to find how much the plant grew in one week. Can you see any patterns in the line graph? (Hint: how much did the height increase each day?)

The title tells what the graph is about.

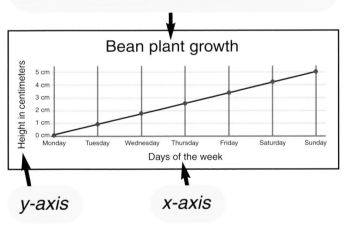

y-axis

x-axis

The axis labels tell about the information on the graph. The days of the week are listed on the x-axis. The y-axis shows the measurements.

BAR GRAPH

This boy did an investigation to find out what kinds of insects live in his backyard. He carefully observed an area in his backyard for one hour. He recorded on a chart the insects he observed. He used the data from his chart to make a bar graph. A bar graph uses bars to compare data about different groups or events.

EXPLORE IT!

Use the bar graph to find out which insect he observed the most. How many insects did he observe altogether? How do you know? How many different kinds of insects did he observe?

My backyard insect observations

Number of insects

ladybug   butterfly   honeybee   mosquito   grasshopper

Types of insects

PICTURE THIS!

Scientists also use diagrams and photographs to share information. They can show information that is difficult to describe using only words.

DIAGRAMS

A diagram is a drawing that shows how something works or how parts go together.

This diagram shows how each part of a plant helps it survive.

The words next to each part are called captions. Captions help give information about each part of a diagram.

Plant parts

Flowers make seeds.

Leaves take in sunlight to make food.

The stem carries water from the roots to the rest of the plant. It also helps keep the plant standing up.

Roots take in water from the soil. Roots also help hold the plant in place.

PHOTOGRAPHS

A photograph is an image created using a camera. These photographs show lightning during a storm. They help us understand what lightning looks like. We can use the details in these photographs to learn that lightning happens during stormy weather.

EXPLORE IT!

?

The diagram shows the position of a honeybee's body parts. Use the diagram to answer the following questions: How many legs are on each side of the insect's body? Which is larger, the thorax or the abdomen? Think of another question that can be answered using this diagram.

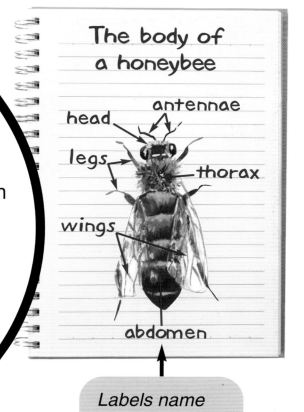

The body of a honeybee

antennae
head
legs
thorax
wings
abdomen

Labels name each body part.

17

WRITE LIKE A SCIENTIST

Scientists often share information through writing. They write reports. A science report usually includes:

- The question you tested
- The steps you followed in your investigation
- Your data
- Any charts, graphs, or diagrams you made
- Your conclusion, or the results shown by your data

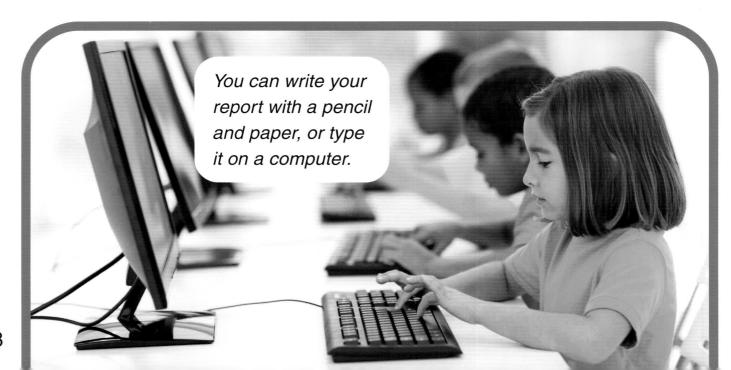

You can write your report with a pencil and paper, or type it on a computer.

TIPS

Scientists share the steps they followed during their investigation. They record this information so that other scientists can repeat the investigation. Words such as *first*, *next*, and *last* help tell the order of the steps.

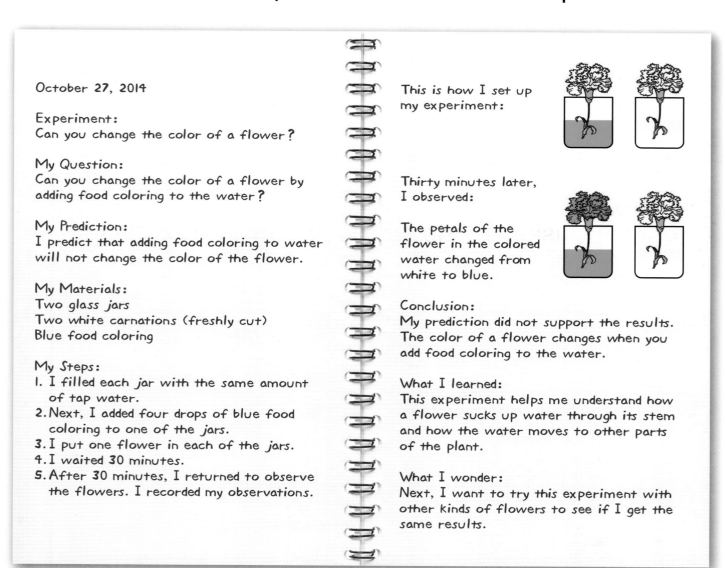

October 27, 2014

Experiment:
Can you change the color of a flower?

My Question:
Can you change the color of a flower by adding food coloring to the water?

My Prediction:
I predict that adding food coloring to water will not change the color of the flower.

My Materials:
Two glass jars
Two white carnations (freshly cut)
Blue food coloring

My Steps:
1. I filled each jar with the same amount of tap water.
2. Next, I added four drops of blue food coloring to one of the jars.
3. I put one flower in each of the jars.
4. I waited 30 minutes.
5. After 30 minutes, I returned to observe the flowers. I recorded my observations.

This is how I set up my experiment:

Thirty minutes later, I observed:

The petals of the flower in the colored water changed from white to blue.

Conclusion:
My prediction did not support the results. The color of a flower changes when you add food coloring to the water.

What I learned:
This experiment helps me understand how a flower sucks up water through its stem and how the water moves to other parts of the plant.

What I wonder:
Next, I want to try this experiment with other kinds of flowers to see if I get the same results.

PRESENT IT!

Scientists also do presentations to share information with others. They talk about their investigations and explain their results so that other people can learn from their work. Presenting your work in front of a group can be a bit scary at first. You can make notes to help you remember important points you want to share.

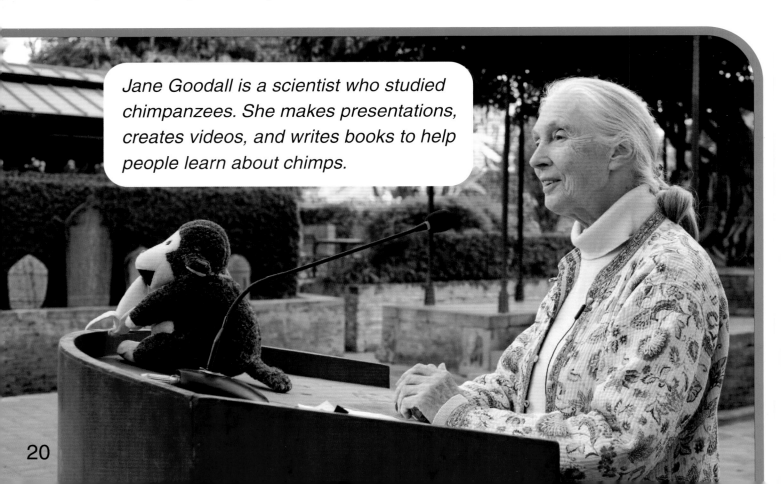

Jane Goodall is a scientist who studied chimpanzees. She makes presentations, creates videos, and writes books to help people learn about chimps.

TALKING TIPS!

Present information using a
clear voice so that everyone
can hear your presentation.
Make eye contact with people.
You can also show posters or
diagrams to help explain your
results. Ask and answer questions.
This is a great opportunity for learning!

EXPLORE IT!

What ideas have you shared
with friends? Did you get
any new ideas from
sharing them?

CITIZEN SCIENTISTS

Would you like to help scientists around the world collect data for their investigations? Join a citizen science project! You can help scientists by collecting information about the environment. You might be asked to count the number of birds you see in your backyard during winter, or record your observations of fireflies.

Ask an adult to help you visit these websites to find a project that is right for you!

http://gbbc.birdcount.org
The Great Backyard Bird Count Citizen scientists tally up the kind and number of birds observed during a certain period in winter.

www.windows2universe.org/ citizen_science/starcount
The Great World Wide Star Count—Citizen scientists observe and record the stars they see in certain constellations.

https://legacy.mos.org/ fireflywatch
Firefly Watch—Citizen scientists share their firefly observations, including habitat information, with local scientists.

http://projectsquirrel.org
Project Squirrel—Citizen scientists share their squirrel observations and can upload photographs.

LEARNING MORE

BOOKS

It's Not Too Late, Let's Communicate by Kelly Doudna. Sandcastle, 2006.

Meeting Dolphins: My Adventures in the Sea by Kathleen Dudzinski. National Geographic Society, 2000.

What Do We Know Now? Drawing Conclusions and Answering the Question by Robin Johnson. Crabtree, 2009.

WEBSITES

This website contains games, videos, and more. Try some of the hands-on investigations described on this website and share your findings with others!
www.wonderville.ca/browse/ fun_science?pid=4

This website features age-appropriate investigations and opportunities for citizen science projects.
www.tvokids.com/shows/ citizenscience

Try one of the many hands-on investigations found on this website. Don't forget to share with a friend what you find out!
www.sciencebob.com/experiments

GLOSSARY

Note: Some boldfaced words are defined where they appear in the text.

experts (EK-spurtz) noun People who know a lot about a topic

graphic organizers (GRAF-ik AWR guh nahy-zerz) noun Charts used to show order or to sort data to compare it

investigate (in-ves-ti-GEYT) verb To take actions step by step to find the answer to a science question

natural world (NACH-er-uhl WURLD) noun All living and non-living things in the world

observations (ob-zur-VEY-shuhnz) noun Things learned by using the senses

observe (ob-zur-V) verb To gather information using your senses.

record (ri-KAWRD) verb To write or put down data in notebooks

scientists (SAHY-uhn-tistz) noun People who learn about the natural world

senses (SENS-uhz) noun Sight, touch, hearing, taste, and smell

A *noun* is a person, place, or thing.
A *verb* is an action word that tells you what someone or something does.

INDEX

citizen scientists 22
communicating 10–11
diagrams 16–17
experiments 7, 9, 19
graphic organizers
  12–13

graphs 14–15
investigations 7, 8, 10, 11, 12, 15, 19, 20
making notes 8–9
photographs 16
predictions 7, 19

presentations 20–21
questions 5, 6, 7, 8, 11, 13
recording information
  12–13
writing reports 18–19